# THE ELECTORAL COLLEGE

## PHIL CORSO

**PowerKiDS**
press.

New York

Published in 2020 by The Rosen Publishing Group, Inc.
29 East 21st Street, New York, NY 10010

First Edition

Editor: Rachel Gintner
Book Design: Tanya Dellaccio

Photo Credits: Cover Joe Amon/Denver Post/Getty Images; p. 5 Drew Angerer/Getty Images News/ Getty Images; p. 7 (Signing of Constitution) https://upload.wikimedia.org/wikipedia/commons/9/9d/ Scene_at_the_Signing_of_the_Constitution_of_the_United_States.jpg ; p. 7 (U.S. Constitution) https:// upload.wikimedia.org/wikipedia/commons/6/6c/Constitution_of_the_United_States%2C_page_1.jpg; pp. 8, 17 Chip Somodevilla/Getty Images News/Getty Images; p. 9 Anadolu Agency/Getty Images; p. 11 Tom Williams/CQ-Roll Call Group/Getty Images; p. 12 Encyclopaedia Britannica/Universal Images Group/Getty Images; p. 13 Bloomberg/Getty Images; p. 15 (Ronald Reagan) Wally McNamee/ Corbis Historical/Getty Images; p. 15 (Franklin D. Roosevelt) Bettmann/Getty Images; p. 16 (Certificate of Ascertainment) Courtesy of Archives.gov; p. 16 (Congressional pages) Bill Clark/CQ-Roll Call Group/Getty Images; p. 19 (Joe Biden) Mark Wilson/Getty Images News/Getty Images; p. 19 (Alexander Hamilton) https://commons.wikimedia.org/wiki/File:Hamilton_Trumbull_1792-retouch.jpg; p. 21 Sarah Rice/Getty Images News/Getty Images; p. 23 Alex Wong/Getty Images News/Getty Images; p. 24 ROBYN BECK/ AFP/Getty Images; p. 25 HENNY RAY ABRAMS/AFP/Getty Images; p. 27 NOVA SAFO/AFP/Getty Images; p. 29 Pacific Press/LightRocket/Getty Images.

Cataloging-in-Publication Data

Names: Corso, Phil.
Title: The electoral college / Phil Corso.
Description: New York : PowerKids Press, 2020. | Series: U.S. presidential elections: how they work | Includes glossary and index.
Identifiers: ISBN 9781725310742 (pbk.) | ISBN 9781725310766 (library bound) | ISBN 9781725310759 (6 pack)
Subjects: LCSH: Electoral college–United States–Juvenile literature. | Presidents–United States–Election–Juvenile literature.
Classification: LCC JK529.C66 2020 | DDC 324.6'3–dc23

Manufactured in the United States of America

CPSIA Compliance Information: Batch # CWPK20. For Further Information contact Rosen Publishing, New York, New York at 1-800-237-9932.

# CONTENTS

# WHAT'S THE ELECTORAL COLLEGE?

In the United States of America, the Electoral College is the way voters elect their president and vice president every four years. In this case, the word "college" refers to the electors who ultimately cast the final votes after every presidential election.

Contrary to popular belief, American voters are not actually casting **ballots** for their preferred candidates directly. Instead, because of the Electoral College, they're voting for their electors, who get appointed by political parties and represent voters later in the year. For example, if you vote for a president and vice president on Election Day in November, and those candidates win the popular vote in your state, your party-chosen electors will then vote for the same candidates. They vote the second Wednesday in December.

American voters head to the polls every four years to **contemplate** and select their president and vice president, but it's actually through the Electoral College that a winner is chosen.

# PATH TO THE PRESIDENCY

UNDER NORMAL CIRCUMSTANCES, PRESIDENTIAL ELECTIONS IN THE UNITED STATES OF AMERICA TYPICALLY OCCUR EVERY FOUR YEARS ON THE TUESDAY AFTER THE FIRST MONDAY IN NOVEMBER.

# THE FOUNDERS' COLLEGE

This system of voting dates as far back as the United States Constitution. When the Founding Fathers established the nation's laws, they landed on the Electoral College as a compromise to satisfy both average citizens and their elected representatives in the college. Under this compromise, voters could select their preferred candidates, while Congress could also play a role in selecting the president and vice president by a popular vote of its own.

The Founders wrote in Article II, Section 1 of the Constitution that each state "shall appoint … a number of electors, equal to the whole number of senators and representatives to which the state may be entitled in the Congress." Those electors would meet in their states to cast their votes.

While drafting the U.S. Constitution, the Founders grappled over how citizens would select their leaders. The Electoral College received the most support because it was viewed as a way of preventing an unhealthy concentration of power.

## FOUNDED ON COMPROMISE

THE ELECTORAL COLLEGE WAS NOT THE ONLY VOTING METHOD CONSIDERED DURING THE CONSTITUTIONAL CONVENTION OF 1787. THE FOUNDERS WERE TORN OVER WHO SHOULD HAVE THE FINAL SAY IN WHO GETS ELECTED PRESIDENT AND VICE PRESIDENT. THEY WONDERED WHETHER IT SHOULD BE CONGRESS, STATE GOVERNORS, STATE **LEGISLATURES**, OTHER ELECTED OFFICIALS, OR SOLELY THE VOTERS THEMSELVES. A COMMITTEE AT THE TIME EVENTUALLY ESTABLISHED THE ELECTORAL COLLEGE TO ACT AS A COMPROMISE.

**U.S. CONSTITUTION**

# ELECTORS' ROLE IN U.S. DEMOCRACY

Electors are usually selected at their respective party's state conventions, and they're typically state leaders, party leaders, or active citizens with strong ties to the presidential candidates. Once selected, these electors cast their ballots for their candidates depending on who wins the popular vote in their respective states. However, it's not set in stone to be this way.

United States House Clerk staff verifies the official 2016 Electoral College votes from Illinois during a joint session of Congress at the U.S. Capitol in Washington, D.C.

The U.S. Constitution does not require electors to vote for their party's candidate, but more than half of the states have laws that do compel them to do so if their party's candidate wins their state's popular vote. In the states that do not have such a law on the books, electors have still followed tradition by voting for their party's nominee after Election Day, nevertheless.

# EVEN THIS COLLEGE HAS RULES

There are rules in the Constitution that govern who could be an elector, how they're selected, and how they must confer. Congress determines when states pick their electors and when they cast their votes for president and vice president. That day is always the same day for the entire country.

The Fourteenth Amendment says that electors cannot be citizens who have "previously taken an oath, as a member of Congress, or as an officer in the United States, or as a member of any state Legislature, or as an executive or judicial officer of any State, to support the Constitution of the United States, shall have engaged in **insurrection** or rebellion against the same, or given aid or comfort to the enemies thereof."

## PATH TO THE PRESIDENCY

THE NUMBER OF ELECTORS THAT EACH STATE GETS CAN CHANGE OVER TIME THROUGH A PROCESS CALLED REAPPORTIONMENT, WHICH DEPENDS ON OFFICIAL CENSUS RESULTS RECORDED EVERY 10 YEARS.

An aide tends to Electoral College ballot boxes during a joint session of Congress in January 2017.

# COLLEGE BY THE NUMBERS

Each of the 50 states receives one elector for every representative in Congress, which is based on how many people live there. They also receive two more for each state's senators. There are 538 electoral votes, and it takes at least 270 of them to win the presidency.

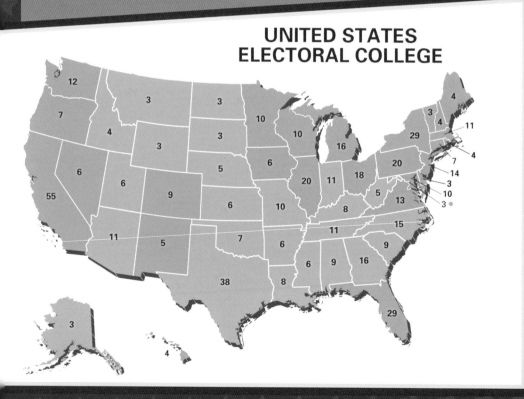

**UNITED STATES ELECTORAL COLLEGE**

Presidential elections can become somewhat of a numbers game, tallying up the electoral votes from each state until one candidate reaches 270 of the 538 total available votes.

The number of electors each state receives ranges anywhere from three, such as Wyoming, to 55, such as California, depending on the size of the states. The Twenty-third **Amendment** of the U.S. Constitution also **allocates** three electors to the District of Columbia, treating it like an actual state.

Most states will give all their electoral votes to one candidate in a winner-take-all fashion, depending on who wins that state. Some states, such as Maine and Nebraska, however, split theirs up.

# "PROPORTIONAL REPRESENTATION"

The Constitution does not say how states should dole out electoral votes. **Proportional** representation is the system used in Maine and Nebraska, where electoral votes are split up proportionally based on vote totals, rather than awarding all the state's votes to whichever candidate wins that state's popular vote. Under the current system, however, this method is somewhat **inconsequential**. Maine and Nebraska have four and five electoral votes respectively.

Critics of the Electoral College have argued that forcing all states to allocate electoral votes through proportional representation could help level the playing field in elections by making certain big-vote states less powerful in selecting the next president and giving more power to smaller states that consistently go toward the same party every four years.

## PATH TO THE PRESIDENCY

MOST STATES GIVE ALL THE AVAILABLE ELECTORAL VOTES TO THE CANDIDATE WHO WINS ITS POPULAR VOTE. BUT A DIFFERENT SYSTEM CALLED PROPORTIONAL REPRESENTATION CHANGES THAT IN TWO STATES, CURRENTLY.

# THE BIGGEST WINS IN ELECTORAL COLLEGE HISTORY

THE 1984 ELECTION OF REPUBLICAN RONALD REAGAN REMAINS THE MOST COMMANDING COLLECTION OF ELECTORAL VOTES IN U.S. HISTORY, WITH REAGAN WINNING 525 OF THE 538 TOTAL ELECTORAL VOTES, DEFEATING DEMOCRAT WALTER MONDALE. ANOTHER NOTEWORTHY VICTORY INCLUDES DEMOCRAT FRANKLIN DELANO ROOSEVELT'S 523 VOTES, OR 97.2 PERCENT OF THE 538 TOTAL VOTES, DEFEATING REPUBLICAN CANDIDATE ALFRED M. LANDON IN 1936.

FRANKLIN D. ROOSEVELT

RONALD REAGAN

# WHEN ELECTORS ELECT

The governors of each state prepare a document called a Certificate of Ascertainment after each presidential election outlining the state's winning candidate and which electors will represent them at a meeting held in December. Those certificates are sent to Congress and the National Archives.

**CERTIFICATE OF ASCERTAINMENT**

## PATH TO THE PRESIDENCY

A MODEL SIMILAR TO THE U.S. ELECTORAL COLLEGE WAS USED DURING THE MIDDLE AGES, WHEN LEADERS OF THE HOLY ROMAN EMPIRE VOTED THROUGH A COLLEGE OF "PRINCE-ELECTORS" FROM GERMAN STATES.

The last stop for Electoral College ballots is in the United States House chamber, where elected officials tally the final results.

Come meeting time, electors get together on either the first Monday or second Wednesday in December after the big vote and cast their votes for president and vice president on two separate ballots. The votes are compiled in a Certificate of Vote, which is also sent to Congress and the National Archives. The votes are then counted in a joint session of Congress during the first week of January, and members of the House and Senate meet to officially tally them.

# WHO ELECTS THE ELECTORS?

Selecting electors is a two-part process. Political parties pick electors in their states before the election, and then after votes are tallied, voters pick them by casting ballots for president. In the first part, the rules depend on the state. Electors are picked at state party conventions or are voted on by political committees. By the end, each presidential candidate has their own list of potential electors.

Nebraska and Maine vary because of proportional representation, and they allow electors to be awarded to more than one candidate. After Election Day, votes are tallied to determine which of those compiled lists gets the green light in the end. Potential electors' names from part one of the process might even appear on the ballot, depending on the state.

Former Vice President Joe Biden and House Speaker Paul Ryan conduct a final count of the Electoral College votes in the House chamber in January 2016.

## THE POWER OF SEPARATING POWERS

IN HIS ESSAY "FEDERALIST NUMBER 68," FOUNDING FATHER ALEXANDER HAMILTON EXPLAINED WHY HE SUPPORTED THE ELECTORAL COLLEGE, ARGUING THAT IT WAS IMPORTANT TO SAFEGUARD THE SACREDNESS OF PRESIDENTIAL ELECTIONS BY LEAVING THE DECISIONS WITH "MEN MOST CAPABLE OF ANALYZING THE QUALITIES ADAPTED TO THE STATION, AND ACTING UNDER CIRCUMSTANCES FAVORABLE TO DELIBERATION, AND TO A JUDICIOUS COMBINATION OF ALL THE REASONS AND INDUCEMENTS WHICH WERE PROPER TO GOVERN THEIR CHOICE."

# WHAT CAN'T THEY DO?

Different states have different rules concerning how electors conduct themselves throughout a presidential election. The U.S. Constitution does not require electors to vote in any particular direction, for example, but some states have laws that say electors are required to vote the same way as the people who voted for them. Meaning, if you're an elector for the Democratic candidate and your candidate wins the election, you must cast your vote for them.

In states where this law is not on the books, electors can "go **rogue**" and vote for a different candidate in the end. However, that sort of action is highly unusual and unlikely. In some instances, electors are bound by pledges to political parties to cast their vote for a certain candidate.

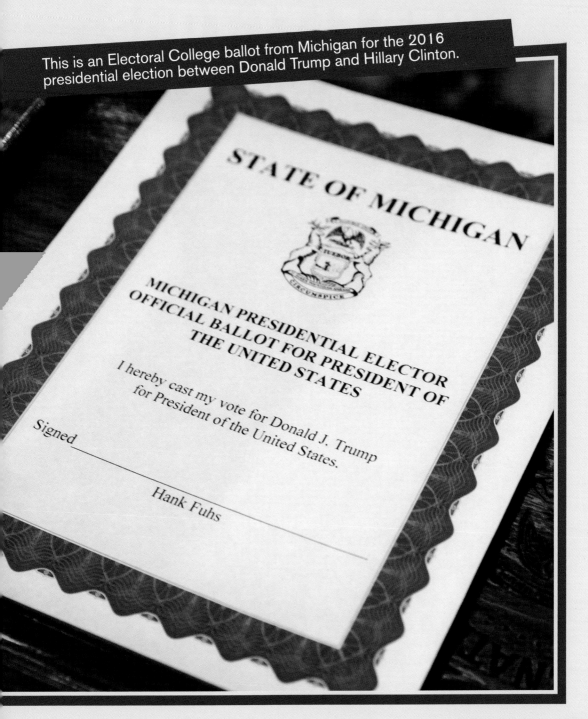

This is an Electoral College ballot from Michigan for the 2016 presidential election between Donald Trump and Hillary Clinton.

STATE OF MICHIGAN

MICHIGAN PRESIDENTIAL ELECTOR
OFFICIAL BALLOT FOR PRESIDENT OF
THE UNITED STATES

I hereby cast my vote for Donald J. Trump
for President of the United States.

Signed _____

Hank Fuhs

# WHEN ELECTORS AREN'T ENOUGH

The Founders did include a special **stipulation** over what to do in the event of a tie. If none of the presidential candidates earn a majority of the 538 electoral votes available, the decision is then sent to the House of Representatives. Each of the 50 states would get one vote, and a majority, meaning 26, of the states would be needed for a candidate to win.

Members of the Senate, then, would elect the vice president, with one vote per senator. The candidate with a majority of the senators' votes wins. All of this would only occur, of course, after the electors **convene** in December to **ratify** the official tie, just in case any of the electors "go rogue" and vote the other way.

IN GOD WE TRUST

In the event of a tie in the Electoral College, the House of Representatives would need to step in to settle the score.

# WHEN THE ELECTORAL COLLEGE FAILED

While it was designed with fairness in mind, there have been times throughout history when the Electoral College awarded victory to the candidate who actually received fewer votes.

There were five times when a candidate won the popular vote, but lost the election: Andrew Jackson in 1824 (to John Quincy Adams); Samuel Tilden in 1876 (to Rutherford B. Hayes); Grover Cleveland in 1888 (to Benjamin Harrison); Al Gore in 2000 (to George W. Bush); Hillary Clinton in 2016 (to Donald J. Trump).

HILLARY CLINTON

DONALD J. TRUMP

Congress considered amending the process in the late 1960s by proposing to switch the process to direct elections that would require a runoff when no candidate **surpasses** a threshold of 40 percent of the vote. But the legislation died in the Senate in 1969.

The 2000 presidential election between George W. Bush and Al Gore was one of five times the candidate with the most votes did not win the election.

GEORGE W. BUSH

AL GORE

# PATH TO THE PRESIDENCY

ELECTORS WHO CHANGE THEIR VOTES ARE CALLED "FAITHLESS ELECTORS." DURING THE 2016 ELECTION, SEVEN ELECTORS BROKE WITH THEIR STATES ON THE PRESIDENTIAL BALLOT AND SIX DID THE SAME FOR VICE PRESIDENT.

# WHY PEOPLE LIKE THE COLLEGE

One of the driving principles behind the Electoral College was to protect the rights of smaller states in the union so that their voices can be heard among the bigger, more populous states. This kind of indirect election process keeps the biggest states in the country, such as California, from becoming too powerful in the voting booth.

Defenders of the Electoral College have argued that it is more important to have political support evenly distributed across the states, rather than solely concentrated in states with the most people. The system also allows more room for minority groups to keep a seat at the table instead of being drowned out completely. Under this system, voters in smaller states have an incentive to vote.

Voters wait in line at their polling place in Michigan.

# WHY PEOPLE DON'T LIKE THE COLLEGE

Calls to abolish the Electoral College have **fluctuated** over the years, but they tend to be loudest when the winner loses the popular vote. The 2016 election was one of those cases, and therefore, public debate over getting rid of the Electoral College has been rekindled.

Those in favor of switching to direct democracy, meaning "one person, one vote," have argued that the federal election process should mirror that of the states, where popular vote determines the winner.

The fact that no state uses an Electoral College for its governor suggests that many standard arguments for the Electoral College—recount nightmares, fairness for rural areas, etc.—are "makeweight," or unjustified, according to Yale University professor Akhil Reed Amar in a *New York Times* opinion piece from November 2016.

Some protesters were angry about the Electoral College after the 2016 election, when President Donald J. Trump lost the popular vote but won the presidency.

## PATH TO THE PRESIDENCY

THE LAST TIME A THIRD-PARTY CANDIDATE WON A STATE'S ELECTORAL VOTES WAS 1968, WHEN GEORGE WALLACE WON FIVE STATES, OR 46 ELECTORAL VOTES, AGAINST RICHARD NIXON AND HUBERT HUMPHREY.

# CAN IT BE IMPROVED?

One of the most common ways to either get rid of, or improve, the Electoral College would be through establishing a constitutional amendment. And because that process could be very long and quarrelsome, it has very rarely even been considered as a way to improve the system.

But there are other ways the nation could build upon the existing method of electing a president. Some have suggested making every state a "winner take all" system, meaning the candidate with a majority of the popular vote wins all of that state's electoral votes. Making this rule apply to all 50 states would also not require a constitutional amendment. Third-party advocates, however, argued that doing so would ultimately eliminate any chance for them to win.

The Electoral College is embedded in the way the United States chooses its leaders, but that does not mean it cannot be improved, perhaps through a constitutional amendment, some say.

# GLOSSARY

**allocate:** To distribute for a particular purpose.

**amendment:** A small change, or addition, to an existing piece of work.

**ballots:** The method used to count someone's vote.

**contemplate:** To view or consider with attention; to reflect on.

**convene:** Coming together for a meeting or activity.

**fluctuate:** To shift back and forth, sometimes uncertainly.

**inconsequential:** Not important.

**insurrection:** An uprising against an authority or a government.

**legislature:** An official body that writes laws for a country or state.

**proportional:** Corresponding with the amount of something else.

**ratify:** To formally approve.

**rogue:** Being dishonest, or going against the norm.

**stipulation:** A condition, requirement, or legal item specified.

**surpass:** To become greater, better, or stronger than.

# INDEX

# WEBSITES

Due to the changing nature of Internet links, PowerKids Press has developed an online list
of websites related to the subject of this book. This site is updated regularly.
Please use this link to access the list: www.powerkidslinks.com/uspe/electoral